THE FIRST
THOUSAND
WORDS
IN SPANISH

First published in 1979
Usborne Publishing Ltd
Usborne House, 83-85 Saffron Hill
London EC1N 8RT, England.
Copyright © 1989 (limp), 1979
Usborne Publishing Ltd.

The name Usborne and the device are
Trade Marks of Usborne Publishing Ltd.

Printed in Great Britain

About this book

This book is for everyone who is starting to learn Spanish. By looking at the pictures, it will be easy to read and learn the words with them. And seeing them in a scene where you would expect to find them, will help you to remember them.

Masculine and feminine words

When you look at the words in Spanish, you will see that most of them have **la** or **el,** which mean 'the', in front of them. When learning Spanish, it is a good idea to learn the **la** or **el** with each word. This is because all Spanish words, like book and table, as well as man and woman, are masculine or feminine. **La** usually means the word is feminine and **el** that it is masculine. If the word is plural—that is, there is more than one thing, such as tables or books, then it has **las** or **los** in front of it. **Las** is the feminine and **los** is the masculine.

Looking at the words

Some Spanish words have an **n** in them with a squiggle over it, like this **ñ**. It is called a tilde. In Spanish this **ñ** is a separate letter of the alphabet and is said differently from the ordinary **n**. Some letters also have accents on them. This does not change the sound of the letter but changes the way the word is spoken.

Saying the words

At the back of the book there is a guide to pronouncing every word in the pictures. This is to help you say them. But there are some sounds in Spanish which are quite different from any sounds in English. To say them as a Spanish person would, you have to hear them spoken. Listen very carefully and then try to say them like that yourself. But if you say them as they are written in the pronunciation guide, a Spanish person will understand you—even if your Spanish accent is not quite perfect.

Spot the duck
There is a duck on every double-page picture. Can you find it?

THE FIRST THOUSAND WORDS IN SPANISH

With Easy Pronunciation Guide

Heather Amery and Reyes Milá
Illustrated by Stephen Cartwright

Pronunciation Guide by Judy Klavans, MED, MA

La casa

el baño

el jabón

el grifo

la espuma
de baño

el cepillo
de dientes

el agua

la toalla

la esponja

la ducha

la pasta
de dientes

el lavabo

el retrete

la biblioteca

la mesita

la radio

el radiador

la lana

el papel pintado

el reloj

la alfombra

el cojín

el tocadisc

la lámpara

la cama

la cómoda

el cepillo

la almohada

el guardarropa

la alfombrilla

los cuadros

el edredón

los vestidos

el peine

el espejo

la sábana

las escaleras

la mosca

el colgador de ropa

la araña

silla

las cartas

el teléfono

la telaraña

el periódico

5

En la cocina

la nevera

los vasos

el relój

las cucharas de madera

el delantal

el interruptor

las cacerolas

los platitos

la plancha

el calentador de agua

el fregasuelos

el aspirador

el fregadero

los tenedores

la puerta

el trapo

el taburete

los cuchillos

la cera dè lu

6

la cocina

los azulejos

el cajón

la basura

la sartén

la lavadora

el recogedor del polvo

los platos

la tabla de planchar

el detergente

el cepillo

la mesa

la bombilla

las tazas

las cucharas

las cerillas

la llave

la escoba

las escudillas

el armario

7

En el jardín

la carretilla

la colmena

el caracol

los ladrillos

el cubo
de basura

la oruga

la pala

la hormiga

el pájaro

el canalón del
tejado

la escalera
de mano

las semillas

el cobertizo

el gusano

las flores

el irrigador

el hueso

el seto

la paleta

el cortacésped

el camino

el árbol

la horca

las hojas

la escoba

la manguera

la azada

el humo

la abeja

el rastrillo

el cochecito de niño

la avispa

las plantas

la hierba

la hoguera

el nido de pájaro

los palos

el invernadero

9

El taller

el papel de lija

el taladro

los tornillos a tuerca

las tachuelas

la sierra

el serrín

el martillo

la lima

la caja de herramientas

el destornillador

el tablón

el bote de pintura

las virutas

la nava

10

el barril

el hacha

las tuercas

la cinta
de medir

los tornillos

la escalera
de mano

los clavos

el torno
de banco

el cepillo
de carpintero

la leña

el banco

los potes

la madera

11

la gasolinera

la ambulancia

la bicicleta

el agujero

el bar

la acera

la tienda

el semáforo

la chimenea

el camión

el paso de peatones

los escalones

el hombre

La calle

el hotel

el coche de policía

la apisonadora

la taladradora

la escuela

el patio de recreo

los pis

12

la estatua

el autobús

el taxi

el remolque

las tuberías

el tejado

el mercado

la fábrica

la antena
de televisión

la furgoneta

el policía

el coche de
bomberos

la casa

la mujer

la iglesia

el cine

el coche

la motocicleta

el conductor

el farol

cavadora

La juguetería

el piano

los naipes

la casa de muñecas

el caramillo

el robot

la armónica

las bolas

el cañón

la máquina fotográfica

las cuentas

el silbato

el cohete

los dados

las muñecas

los cosmonautas

el caballo de balancín

la grúa

la apisonadora

las paletas de tenis

la guitarra

la caja de herramientas

14

la caña de pescar

la caja de pinturas

la arcilla

el paracaídas

la máquina de escribir

el yate

el blanco

el tanque

los soldaditos de plomo

el fuerte

la hucha

aja de tren

los títeres

las máscaras

el arco y las flechas

el submarino

los tambores

las pelotas

el coche de carreras

la trompeta

la escopeta

15

El parque

la pelota

la cuerda

el hoyo de arena

el picnic

la cometa

el helado

el perro

los columpios

la verja

el sendero

los renacuajos

el tobogán

16

la rana

el matorral

los patines
de ruedas

los niños

el patin

los cisnes

el bebé

la tierra

las vallas

la sillita de ruedas

las palomas

el columpio

las flores

el charco

los patitos

la cuerda de saltar

el barquito

macizo de flores

el banco

el lago

la correa de perro

los patos

los árboles 17

En el zoo

el panda

el murciélago

el pingüino

el hipopótamo

el ala

las patas

el canguro

el águila

las plumas

el avestruz

el lobo

el mono

el pelícano

la jirafa

el gorila

el oso

el castor

el león

los cachorros de león

el cocodrilo

los cuernos

el ciervo

el camello

la foca

el oso blanco

os monos

la trompa

la zebra

el elefante

el búfalo

el rinoceronte

el tiburón

el rabo

las cabras

el delfín

el leopardo

la ballena

el tigre

19

La estación de ferrocarril

los raíles

el jefe de estación

la máquina

los topes

el vagón restaurante

los vagones

el maquinista

el tren de mercancías

el andén

las señales

el revisor

El garaje

las maletas

las luces delanteras

el motor

la aceitera

la batería

el camión de gasolina

20

El aeropuerto

la azafata

el helicóptero

la pista de aterrizaje

el avión

la torre de control

el piloto

el lavado de coches

el portaequipajes

la bomba de aire

rueda

la llave inglesa

el neumático

el capó

la grúa

el aceite

el surtidor de gasolina

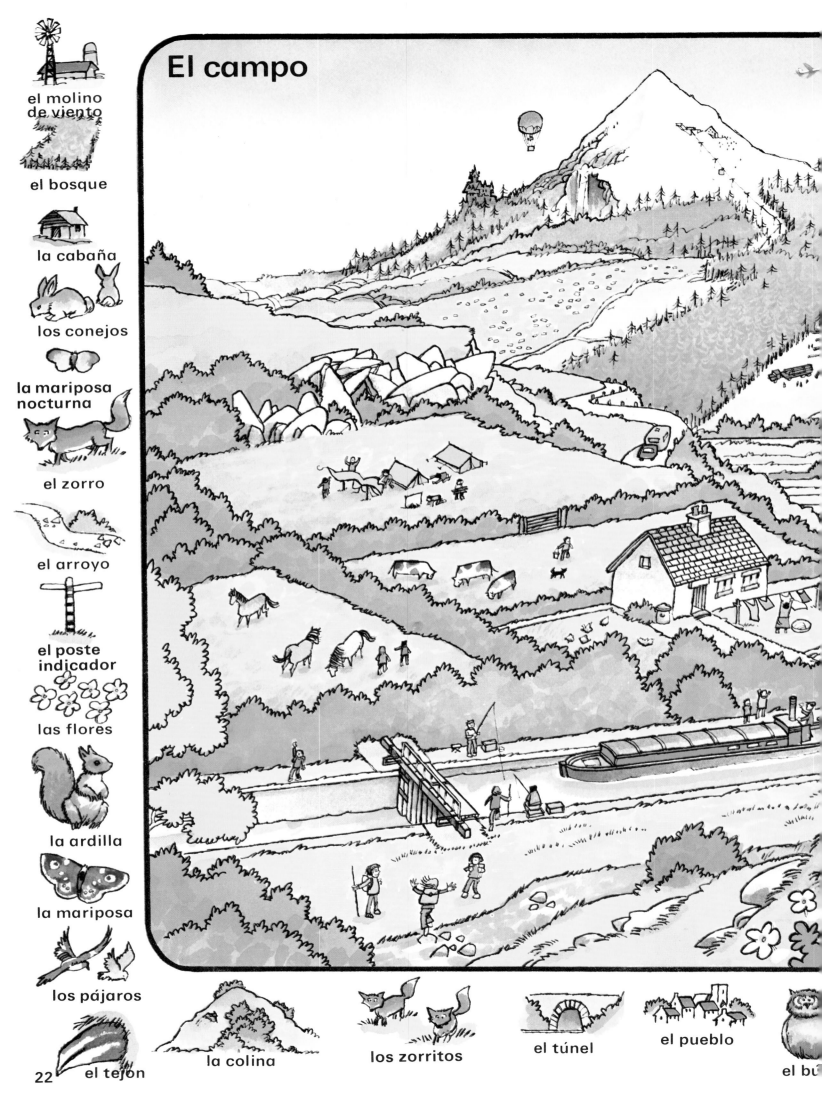

El campo

el molino de viento

el bosque

la cabaña

los conejos

la mariposa nocturna

el zorro

el arroyo

el poste indicador

las flores

la ardilla

la mariposa

los pájaros

el tejón

la colina

los zorritos

el túnel

el pueblo

el bú

22

el globo

la caravana

los troncos

las tiendas de campaña

la carretera

el puente

la barcaza

la cascada

la montaña

las piedras

el topo

la puerta de esclusa

el pescador

las rocas

el canal

el tren

el río

23

La granja

el estanque

las ovejas

el almiar

los patos

el remolque

los corderos

la valla

el pajar

la pocilga

el toro

el lodo

los cerditos

el granero

la cuadra

el granjero

la carreta

el pony

el tractor

la silla de montar

las ocas

las balas de paja

los saca

24

el camión

el huerto

el gallinero

el establo

la vaca

los patitos

el gallo

el ternero

el arado

el perro pastor

el pastor

los pavos

el espantapájaros

la granja

los cerdos

los pollitos

el caballo

los ansarinos

el heno

el campo

el trigo

gallinas

25

La playa

el barco
de vela

el mar

el remo

el faro

la pala

el cubo

la estrella
de mar

el castillo
de arena

la gaviota

la bandera

el cangrejo

el marinero

el sombrero
de paja

la boya

la isla

el puerto

la tumbona

la lancha
de motor

el esquiador acuátic

las olas

la concha
de mar

el acantilado

el barco

la canoa

las
piedrecitas

el balón

las rocas

las aletas

el alga

la red

el canalete

la barca
de pesca

uitasol

el burro

el petrolero

el bote de remos

el traje
de baño

la cuerda

La escuela

la pecera

la placa

el techo

los lápices

los chicos

el calendario

la pared

la papelera

las tijeras

4+2 =
3−2 =

las cuentas

la regla

el pupitre

las fotos

28

las pinturas

el papel

los pinceles

la campanilla

a b c ch d e f
g h i j k l ll m
n ñ o p q r rr s
t u v w x y z

el abecedario

las cajas

los libros

a b c ch d e f g h i
j k l ll m n ñ o p q
r rr s t u v w x y z

el cuadro

las plumas

la tiza

el caballete

el suelo

las plantas

las chicas

el globo
terráqueo

la cola

el pomo de
la puerta

el cuaderno

las chinchetas

dibujo

el mapa

los lápices
de colores

la lámpara

la pizarra

la persiana

la goma

la profesora

29

En el hospital

la camilla

las muletas

el algodón

el osito de trapo

el ascensor

el vaso

el portero

la bata

las píldoras

la enfermera

la bandeja

las flores

la cortina

el tebeo

el termómetro

la muñeca

el r

30

el armario de cabecera

las medicinas

las zapatillas

el pijama

la inyección

el zumo

el camisón

el armario

la televisión

el rompecabezas

cama

la gráfica de temperaturas

el enyesado

la venda

el ojo morado

la silla de ruedas

el médico 31

La fiesta

los globos

las bengalas

los sombreros
de papel

el dulce
de crema

los bocadillos

la luna

los caramelos

las galletas

32

el mantel

los discos

el pastel

el chocolate

los bollos

la lintern

los juguetes

la cinta

las velas

las pajitas

las estrellas

los paquetes

el budín

los regalos

la ventana

la jalea

los fuegos artificiales

la guirnalda de papel

el disfraz

33

los plátanos

las toronjas

la lechuga

las uvas

la coliflor

las manzanas

las zanahorias

los puerros

la calabaza

el pepino

los limones

el apio

las judías

las cerezas

los albaricoques

la col

el melón

El supermercado

QUESO

CARNE

FRUTA

FRUTA

VERDURAS

los champiñones

las cebollas

los tomates

los melocotones

los guisantes

la piña

las ciruelas

las patatas

las frambuesas

las espinacas

34

PESCADO

PAN

COMESTIBLES

las latas

el pan

la mantequilla

el queso

el pollo

los huevos

el pescado

la harina

la compota

la carne

las salchichas

el yogur

el cesto

las botellas

s de Bruselas

las naranjas

las fresas

las bolsas

la caja

la balanza

el dinero

el monedero

el carrito

el bolso

35

Los alimentos

el desayuno

la comida

el café

el pollo

la mermelada

los huevos fritos

la leche

la miel

el chocolate caliente

las chuletas

la crema

la cerveza

el jamón

la sal

la pimienta

36

le cena

el té

las nueces

la carne

el zumo de naranja

la tortilla

la ensalada

el azúcar

la sopa

los panecillos

el arroz

el cocido

las tortitas

el vino

los fideos

la salsa

37

El cuerpo humano

el pelo

la ceja

el ojo

la nariz

la mejilla

la boca

los labios

los dientes

la lengua

la barbilla

el cuello

las orejas

la cabeza

la cara

los hombros

los brazos

el codo

las manos

los dedos

los pulgares

la espalda

el trasero

el pecho

el estómago

las rodillas

las piernas

los pies

los dedos del pie

el talón

Los vestidos

los calzoncillos

la camiseta

los pantalones

los tejanos

la camiseta

la falda

la camisa

la corbata

los pantalones cortos

los calcetines

el suéter

el jersey

la chaqueta

las medias

la blusa

el vestido

las zapatillas de goma

los zapatos

las sandalias

las botas

los guantes

la americana

el anorak

el abrigo

el pañuelo

la gorra

el sombrero

el cinturón

los botones

los ojales

los bolsillos

la cremallera

las hebillas

los cordones

la bufanda

39

La gente

el actor

el cocinero

la bailarina

el carpintero

el submarinista

el astronauta

el director de orquesta

el payaso

el soldado

el policía

el granjero

la cantante

el tendero

el corredor automovilista

el mecánico

el artista

40

el bombero

carnicero

el cartero

el buzo

el maquinista

el pintor

el alpinista

el dentista

el piloto

el juez

el guardián del zoo

el panadero

La familia

el padre
el esposo

la madre
la esposa

la hija
la hermana

el hijo
el hermano

la tía

el tío

el primo

la abuela

el abuelo

Palabras de acción

sonreir

llevar

bañarse

escribir

pensar

partir

andar a gatos

construir

pintar

leer

lavarse los dientes

escuchar

cortar

romper

caerse

lavarse

esconderse

beber

barrer

hacer punto

reirse

llorar

bailar

atrapar

estar sentados

42

trepar

cer pompas

cocinar

jugar

pelear

saltar

coseinar

dormir

esperar

mirar

lanzar

hablar

tomar

comer

coser

tirar

cantar

ganar

correr

saltar

cavar

hacer

star de pie

comprar

andar

empujar

43

Palabras opuestas

pequeño

grande

gordo

delgad

bueno

malo

mitad

todo

frío

caliente

arriba

blando

duro

abajo

primero

último

lejos

pocas

much

cerca

vacío

lleno

a la izquierda

alto

bajo

sucio

limpio

44

lento

rápido

fácil

difícil

largo

corto

arriba

abajo

bonito

feo

encima

debajo

la parte delantera

la parte trasera

mojado

seco

vivo

muerto

oscuro

claro

abierto

cerrado

a la derecha

viejo

nuevo

fuera

dentro

Palabras de libros de cuentos

el castillo

el dragón

el caballero

la escoba

la bruja

la pistola

el gigante

el cañón

el pirata

el tesor

la varita mágica

el pozo

la seta

el duende

el enano

el hada

el mago

el desierto

el ladrón

el indio

el sheriff

el vaquero

la diligencia

el demonio

la corona

el paje

la princesa

el príncipe

la espada

la reina

el rey

el palacio

el ángel

el dinosaurio

la cárcel

los renos

el trineo

el Papá Noel

el mago

el fantasma

el novio

la novia

las damas de honor

la boda

el monstruo

Animales favoritos

los conejos

el gato

el perro

los peces

los lagartos

el loro

las ranas

los periquitos

el erizo

los gusanos de seda

el hámster

los sapos

los cachorros

las palomas

los ratones

las culebras

los gatitos

la tortuga

48

Palabras sobre el tiempo

la niebla

la lluvia

la helada

las nubes

la nieve

el sol

el arco iris

el relámpago

el rocío

el viento

la neblina

as estaciones

la primavera

el verano

el otoño

el invierno

Los deportes

el boxeo

el ciclismo

el béisbol

la natación

el fútbol

la gimnasia

el salto de altura

el esquí

la carrera de coches

el tenis

la carrera de caballos

el patinaje

el tiro al blanco

el cricket

el levantamiento de pesos

el concurso hípico

la carrera de motocicletas

la equitación

la navegación

el ping-pong

el remo

la lucha libre

el baloncesto

el judo

Los colores

negro

color naranja

verde

marrón

azul

rojo

color rosa

blanco

morado

gris

amarillo

Las formas

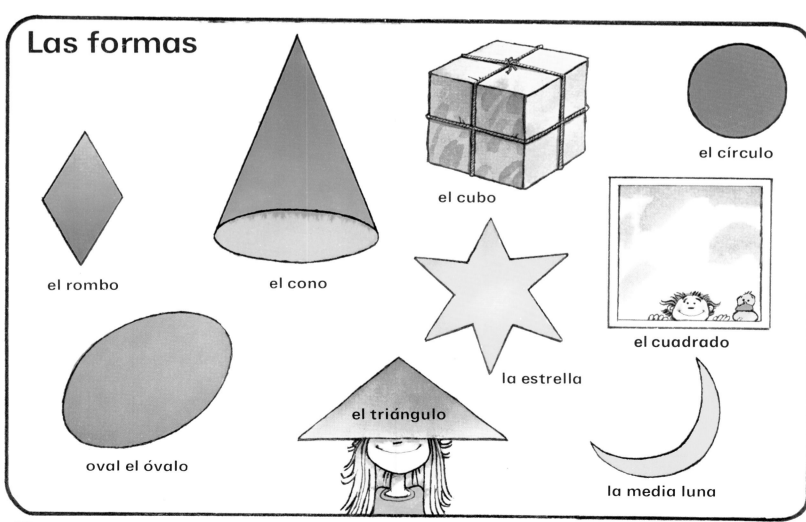

el rombo

el cono

el cubo

el círculo

el cuadrado

la estrella

oval el óvalo

el triángulo

la media luna

Los números

1	uno
2	dos
3	tres
4	cuatro
5	cinco
6	seis
7	siete
8	ocho
9	nueve
10	diez
11	once
12	doce
13	trece
14	catorce
15	quince
16	dieciséis
17	diecisiete
18	dieciocho
19	diecinueve
20	veinte

La feria

el tiovivo

la esterilla

el tobogán

la noria

los coches de choque

la montaña rusa

los aros

las palomitas de maíz

el caramelo americano

el tren fantasma

la barraca de tiro al blanco

El circo

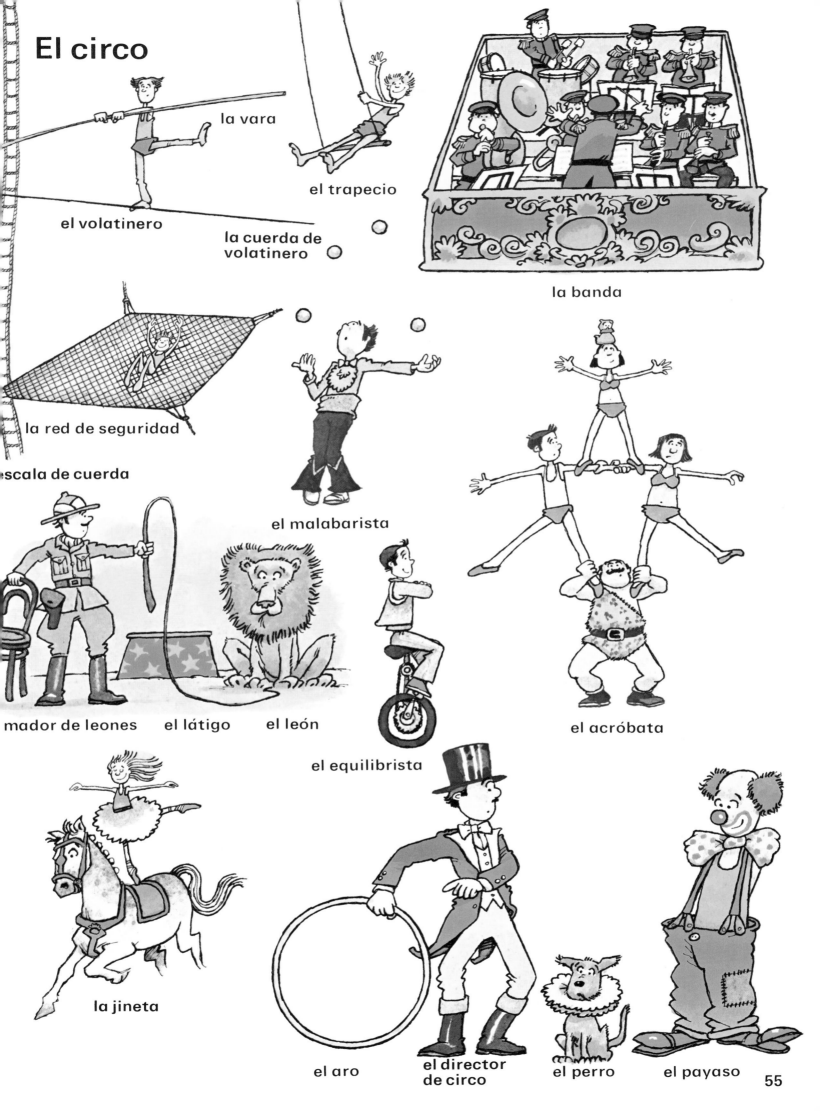

la vara

el volatinero

el trapecio

la cuerda de volatinero

la banda

la red de seguridad

scala de cuerda

el malabarista

mador de leones

el látigo

el león

el equilibrista

el acróbata

la jineta

el aro

el director de circo

el perro

el payaso

55

Index Words in the pictures

This is the alphabetical list of all the words in the pictures in this book. The Spanish word comes first, then there is the pronunciation in *italics*, followed by the English translation.

Although some Spanish words look a little like English ones, they are not pronounced in the same way. In Spanish, when the letter *c* comes before *i* or *e* it sounds like English *th* in *the*.

There are some sounds in the Spanish language which are quite different from any sounds in English. The pronunciation is a guide to help you

say the Spanish words correctly. They may look funny or strange. Just read them as if they are English words, except for these special rules:

> *ah* is said like *a* in *tar*
> *eh* is like *e* in *get*
> *ee* is like *ee* in *feet*
> *oh* is like *o* in *toe*
> *oo* is like *oo* in *pool*
> *r* is made by a flap of the tip of your tongue on the top of your mouth.
> *rr* is said in the same way as a Scotsman rolls the *rr* in the word *merry*.

Spanish	Pronunciation	English
abajo	*ah-bah-gho*	bottom
el abecedario	*el ah-beh-theh-dah-ree-o*	alphabet
la abeja	*lah ah-beh-ghah*	bee
abierto/abierta	*ah-byehr-toe/ ah-byehr-tah*	open
el abrigo	*el ah-bree-go*	coat
la abuela	*lah ah-bweh-lah*	grandmother
el abuelo	*el ah-bweh-lo*	grandfather
el acantilado	*el ah-kahn-tee-lah-tho*	cliff
el aceite	*el ah-theh-ee-teh*	oil
la aceitera	*lah ah-theh-ee-teh-rah*	oil can
la acera	*lah ah-theh-rah*	pavement
el acróbata	*el ah-kro-bah-tah*	acrobat
el actor	*el akt-or*	actor
el aeropuerto	*el ah-ee-ro-pwer-toe*	airport
el agua	*el ah-gwah*	water
el águila	*el ah-gee-lah*	eagle
el agujero	*el ah-goo-gheh-ro*	hole
la ala	*lah ah-lah*	wing
el albaricoque	*el al-bah-ree-ko-keh*	apricot
las aletas	*lahs ah-leh-tahs*	flippers
la alfombra	*lah ahl-foam-bra*	carpet
la alfombrilla	*lah ahl-foam-bree-yah*	rug
el alga	*el ahl-gah*	seaweed
el algodón	*el ahl-go-dohn*	cotton wool
los alimentos	*lohs ah-lee-men-tose*	food
el almiar	*el ahl-mee-yahr*	haystack
el almohada	*el ahl-moh-ah-thah*	pillow
el alpinista	*el ahl-pee-nees-tah*	mountaineer
alto/alta	*ahl-toe/ahl-tah*	high
amarillo	*ah-mah-ree-lyo*	yellow
la ambulancia	*lah ahm-boo-lahn-thee-yah*	ambulance
la americana	*lah ah-meh-ree-kah-nah*	jacket
andar	*ahn-dar*	to walk
andar a gatos	*ahn-dar ah gah-tohs*	to crawl
el andén	*el ahn-then*	platform
el ángel	*el ahn-ghel*	angel
el animal favorito	*el ah-nee-mahl fah-boh-ree-toe*	pet
el anorak	*el ah-noh-rahk*	anorak
el ansarino	*el ahn-sah-ree-noh*	gosling
la antena de televisión	*lah ahn-teh-nah-deh teh-leh-bee-thyone*	aerial
el apio	*el ah-pee-yo*	celery

Spanish	Pronunciation	English
la apisonadora	*lah ah-pee-soh-nah-doh-rah*	steamroller
el arado	*el ah-rah-doe*	plough
la araña	*lah ah-rah-nya*	spider
el árbol	*el ahr-bole*	tree
la arcilla	*lah ar-thee-lyah*	clay
el arco	*el ahr-koh*	bow
el arco iris	*el ahr-koh ee-reese*	rainbow
la ardilla	*lah ar-dee-lyah*	squirrel
el armario	*el ar-maryo*	cupboard
el armario de cabecera	*el ahr-mah-ee-yo deh cah-beh-theh-rah*	bedside locker
la armónica	*lah armoh-nee-kah*	mouthorgan
el aro	*el ah-ro*	hoop
los aros	*los ah-rohs*	hoop-la
arriba	*ah-ree-bah*	top, upstairs
el arroyo	*el ah-roy-yo*	stream
el arroz	*el ah-rothe*	rice
el artista	*el ar-tee-stah*	artist
el ascensor	*el ahs-then-sore*	lift
el aspirador	*el ahs-pee-rah-door*	vacuum cleaner
el astronauta	*el ahs-troh-now-tah*	astronaut
atrapar	*ah-trah-pahr*	to catch
el autobús	*el ah-oo-toe-boos*	bus
el avestruz	*el ah-beh-stroos*	ostrich
el avión	*el ah-byone*	plane
la avispa	*lah ah-bees-pah*	wasp
la azada	*lah ah-thah-dah*	hoe
la azafata	*lah ah-thah-fah-tah*	air hostess
el azúcar	*el ah-thoo-kar*	sugar
azul	*ah-thool*	blue
el azulejo	*el ah-thoo-leh-ghoh*	tile
bailar	*bah-ee-lar*	to dance
la bailarina	*lah bah-ee-lahr-een-ah*	dancer
bajo/baja	*bah-ghoe/bah-ghah*	low
la bala de paja	*lah bah-lah deh paj-ghah*	straw bale
la balanza	*lah bah-lahn-thah*	scales
el balón	*el bah-lone*	balloon, ball
el baloncesto	*el bah-lone-thes-toe*	basketball
la ballena	*lah bah-yeh-nah*	whale
bañarse	*bah-nyar-say*	to bath
el banco	*el bahn-ko*	seat, bench
la banda	*la bahn-dah*	band

56

la bandeja	la bahn-deh-ghah	tray
la bandera	la bahn-deh-rah	flag
el baño	el bah-nyo	bath
el bar	el bahr	café
la barbilla	lah bahr-bee-lyah	chin
la barcaza	lah bahr-kah-thah	barge
el barco	el bahr-ko	boat
la barca de pesca	lah bahr-kah deh pehs-kah	fishing boat
el barco de vela	el bahr-ko deh beh-lah	sailing boat
el barquito	el bahr-kee-toh	toy boat
la barraca de tiro	lah bahr-rah-kah deh	rifle range
el blanco	tee-ro el blahn-ko	
barrer	bah-rehr	to sweep
el barril	el bah-reel	barrel
la basura	lah bah-soo-rah	rubbish
la bata	lah bah-tah	dressing gown
la bateria	lah bah-teh-ree-ah	battery
el bebé	el beh-beh	baby
beber	beh-behr	to drink
la biblioteca	lah bee-blee-yoh-teh-kah	bookcase
la bicicleta	lah bee-thee-kleh-tah	bicycle
el béisbol	el beh-yeese-bole	baseball
la bengala	lah ben-gah-lah	sparkler
blanco/blanca	blahn-ko/blahn-kah	white
el blanco	el blahn-ko	target
blando/blanda	blahn-doe/blahn-dah	soft
la blusa	lah bloo-sah	blouse
la boca	lah boh-kah	mouth
el bocadillo	el boh-kah-dee-lyo	sandwich
la boda	lah boh-dah	wedding
la bola	lah boh-la	marble
el bollo	el boy-yo	bun
la bolsa	lah bole-sah	bag
el bolsillo	el bole-see-lyo	pocket
el bolso	el bole-so	handbag
la bomba de aire	lah bohm-bah deh ah-ee-ray	air pump
el bombero	el bowm-beh-ro	fireman
la bombilla	lah bowm-bee-lyah	light bulb
bonito/bonita	boh-nee-toe/boh-nee-tah	nice
el bosque	el bohs-keh	wood, forest
las botas	lahs boh-tahs	boots
el bote de pintura	el boh-teh deh peen-too-rah	paint pot
el bote de remos	el boh-te deh reh-mos	rowing boat
la botella	lah boh-teh-yah	bottle
el botón	el boh-tone	button
el boxeo	el bok-say-yo	boxing
la boya	lah boy-ya	buoy
el brazo	el brah-tho	arm
la bruja	lah broo-ghah	witch
el budín	el boo-deen	pudding
bueno/buena	bweh-noh/bweh-nah	good
el búfalo	el boo-fah-lo	buffalo
la bufanda	lah boo-fahn-dah	scarf
el buho	el boo-oh	owl
la burbúja	lah boor-boo-ghah	bubble
el burro	el boo-ro	donkey
el buzo	el boo-thoh	deep-sea diver
el caballete	el kah-bah-lyeh-teh	easel
el caballero	el kah-bah-lyeh-ro	knight
el caballo	el kah-bah-lyo	horse
el caballo de balancín	el kah-bah-lyo bah-lahn-theen	rocking horse
la cabaña	la kah-bah-nyah	hut
la cabeza	lah kah-beh-thah	head
la cabra	lah kah-bra	goat
la cacerola	el kah-ther-roh-la	saucepan
el cachorro	el kah-choh-ro	puppy
el cachorro de león	el kah-choh-ro-deh leh-yone	lion cub
caerse	kah-yehr-seh	to fall
el café	el kah-feh	coffee

la caja	lah kah-ghah	cash desk, box
la caja de herramientas	lah kah-ghah deh eh-rah-myen-tahs	tool box
la caja de pinturas	lah kah-ghah deh peen-too-rahs	paint box
la caja de tren	lah kah-ghah deh trehn	train set
el cajón	el kah-ghone	drawer
la calabaza	lah kah-lah-bah-thah	pumpkin
el calcetín	el kahl-theh-teen	sock
el calendario	el kah-len-dah-ree-yo	calendar
el calentador de agua	el kah-len-tah-dor deh ah-gwah	kettle
caliente	kah-lyen-teh	hot
la calle	lah kay-yeh	street
los calzoncillos	lohs kahl-thone-see-lyose	pants
la cama	lah kah-mah	bed
el camello	el kah-meh-lyo	camel
la camilla	lah kah-mee-lyah	trolley
el camino	el kah-mee-no	path
el camión	el kah-mee-yone	lorry
el camión de gasolina	el kah-mee-yone deh gah-so-lee-nah	petrol tanker
la camisa	lah kah-mee-sah	shirt
la camiseta	lah kah-mee-seh-tah	T-shirt, vest
el camisón	el kah-mee-sone	nightdress
la campanilla	lah kam-pah-nee-lyah	bell
el campo	el kahm-po	countryside, field
la caña de pescar	lah kah-nyah deh peh-skahr	fishing rod
el canal	el kah-nahl	canal
el canalete	el kah-nah-let-teh	paddle
el canalón del tejado	el kah-nah-lone del teh-ghah-do	gutter
el cangrejo	el kahn-greh-gho	crab
el canguro	el kahn-goo-ro	kangaroo
la canoa	lah kah-no-ah	canoe
el cañón	el kah-nyone	cannon
la cantante	lah kahn-tahn-teh	singer
cantar	kahn-tahr	to sing
el capó	el kah-po	car bonnet
la cara	lah kah-rah	face
el caracol	el kah-rah-kole	snail
el caramelo	el kah-rah-meh-lo	sweet
el caramelo americano	el kah-rah-meh-lo ah-meh-ree-kah-no	candyfloss
el caramillo	el kah-rah-mee-lyo	recorder
la caravana	lah kah-rah-bah-nah	caravan
la carcel	lah kahr-thel	prison
la carne	lah kar-neh	meat
el carnicero	el kar-nee-theh-roe	butcher
el carpintero	el kar-peen-teh-ro	carpenter
la carrera de motocicletas	lah kah-reh-rah deh moh-toh-thee-kleh-tass	speedway cycling
la carrera de caballos	lah kah-reh-rah deh kah-bah-lyose	horse racing
la carrera de coches	lah kah-reh-rah deh koh-chehs	motor racing
la carreta	lah kah-reh-tah	cart
la carretera	lah kah-reh-teh-rah	road
la carretilla	lah kah-reh-tee-lyah	wheelbarrow
el carrito	el kah-ree-toe	trolley
la carta	lah kar-tah	letter
el cartero	el kar-teh-ro	postman
la casa	lah kah-sah	house
la casa de muñecas	lah kah-sah deh moo-nyeh-kahs	dolls' house
la cascada	lah kahs-kah-dah	waterfall
el castillo	el kah-stee-lyo	castle
el castillo de arena	el kah-stee-lyo deh ah-reh-nah	sandcastle
el castor	el kah-stor	beaver
catorce	kah-tore-theh	fourteen
cavar	kah-bar	to dig
la cebolla	lah theh-bo-lyah	onion
le ceja	lah theh-ghah	eyebrow

Spanish	Pronunciation	English
la cena	*lah theh-nah*	supper, dinner
el cepillo	*el theh-pee-lyo*	brush
el cepillo de carpintero	*el theh-pee-lyoh deh kar-peen-teh-ro*	plane (wood)
el cepillo de dientes	*el theh-pee-lyoh deh dyehn-tehs*	toothbrush
la cera de lustrar	*lah theh-rah deh loo-strahr*	polish
cerca	*thehr-thah*	near
el cerdo	*el thehr-doe*	pig
el cerdito	*el thehr-dee-toe*	piglet
la cereza	*lah theh-reh-thah*	cherry
la cerilla	*lah theh-ree-lyah*	match
cerrado/cerrada	*theh-rah-doh/ theh-rah-dah*	shut
la cerveza	*lah thehr-beh-thah*	beer
el cesto	*el thehs-toe*	basket
el champiñón	*el chomp-ee-nyon*	mushroom
la chaqueta	*lah chah-keh-teh*	cardigan
el charco	*el chahr-ko*	puddle
la chica	*lah chee-kah*	girl
el chico	*el chee-ko*	boy
la chiminea	*lah chee-mee-neh-ah*	chimney
la chincheta	*lah cheen-cheh-tah*	drawing pin
el chocolate	*el choh-koh-lah-teh*	chocolate
el chocolate caliente	*el choh-koh-lah-teh kah-lyen-teh*	hot chocolate
la chuleta	*lah choo-leh-tah*	chop
el ciclismo	*el thee-cleese-moh*	cycling
el ciervo	*el thyehr-bo*	deer
cinco	*theen-koh*	five
el cine	*el thee-neh*	cinema
la cinta	*lah theen-tah*	ribbon
la cinta de medir	*lah theen-tah deh meh-deer*	tape measure
el cinturón	*el theen-too-rone*	belt
el circo	*el theer-ko*	circus
el circulo	*el theer-koo-loh*	circle
la ciruela	*lah theer-roo-eh-lah*	plum
el cisne	*el thees-neh*	swan
claro/clara	*klah-roh/klah-rah*	light
el clavo	*el klah-boh*	nail
el cobertizo	*el koh-behr-tee-thoh*	shed
el coche	*el koh-cheh*	car
el coche bomberos	*el koh-cheh bohm-beh-rohs*	fire engine
el coche de carreras	*el koh-cheh deh kah-reh-rahs*	racing car
los coches de choque	*lohs koh-chehs-deh choh-keh*	dodgems
el coche de policía	*el koh-cheh deh poh-lee-thee-yah*	police car
el cochecito de niño	*el koh-cheh-thee-toe deh nee-nyo*	pram
el cocido	*el koh-thee-doe*	stew
la cocina	*lah koh-thee-nah*	kitchen, cooker
cocinar	*koh-thee-nahr*	to cook
el cocinero	*el koh-thee-neh-ro*	cook
el cocodrilo	*el koh-koh-dree-lo*	crocodile
el codo	*el koh-doe*	elbow
el cohete	*el koh-weh-teh*	rocket
el cojín	*el koh-gheen*	cushion
la col	*lah koll*	cabbage
la cola	*lah koh-lah*	glue
las coles de Bruselas	*lahs koh-lehs deh broo-seh-lahs*	Brussels sprouts
el colgador de ropa	*el kohl-gah-dor deh roh-pah*	peg
la coliflor	*lah koh-lee-flohr*	cauliflower
la colina	*lah koh-lee-nah*	hill
la colmena	*lah kohl-menah*	beehive
el color	*el koh-lore*	colour
color naranja	*koh-lore nah-rahn-ghah*	orange (colour)
color rosa	*koh-lore roh-sah*	pink
el columpio	*el koh-loom-pyo*	see-saw
los columpios	*lohs koh-loom-pyos*	swings
comer	*koh-mehr*	to eat
los comestibles	*los koh-mehs-tee-blehs*	groceries
la cometa	*lah koh-meh-tah*	kite
la comida	*lah koh-mee-dah*	lunch, dinner
la cómoda	*lah koh-moh-dah*	chest-of-drawers
la compota	*la kohm-po-tah*	jam
comprar	*kohm-prahr*	to buy
la concha de mar	*lah kone-chah deh mahr*	sea shell
el concurso de hípico	*el kohn-koor-soh deh ee-pee-koh*	showjumping
el conductor	*el kone-dook-tore*	driver
el conejo	*el kone-eh-gho*	rabbit
el cono	*el koh-no*	cone
construir	*kone-stroo-eer*	to build
la corbata	*lah kor-bah-tah*	tie
el cordero	*el kor-deh-ro*	lamb
el cordón	*el kore-done*	shoelace
la corona	*lah koh-roh-nah*	crown
la correa de perro	*lah koh-ray-yah deh peh-ro*	dog lead
el corredor de automotovilista	*el koh-reh-door deh ah-oo-toe-moh-toh-bee-lee-stah*	racing driver
correr	*koh-rehr*	to run
el cortacésped	*el kohr-tah-thehs-ped*	lawn mower
cortar	*kore-tahr*	to cut
coseinar	*koh-thee-nahr*	to pick (harvest)
la cortina	*lah kor-tee-nah*	curtain
corto/corta	*kor-toe/kor-tah*	short
coser	*koh-sehr*	to sew
el cosmonauto	*kohs-moh-nah-oo-toe*	spaceman
la crema	*lah kreh-mah*	cream
la cremallera	*lah kre-mah-yeh-rah*	zip
el cricket	*el kree-keht*	cricket (sport)
el cuaderno	*el kwah-dehr-no*	notebook
la cuadra	*lah kwa-drah*	stable
el cuadro	*el kwah-dro*	picture
el cuadradro	*el kwah-dra-droh*	square
cuatro	*kwah-tro*	four
el cubo	*el koo-bo*	bucket, block, cube
el cubo de basura	*el koo-bo deh bah-soo-rah*	rubbish bin
la cuchara	*lah koo-chah-rah*	spoon
la cuchara de madera	*lah koo-chah-rah deh mah-deh-rah*	wooden spoon
el cuchillo	*el koo-chee-lyo*	knife
el cuello	*el kweh-lyo*	neck
la cuenta	*lah kwen-tah*	bead, sum
la cuerda	*lah kwehr-dah*	rope
la cuerda de saltar	*lah kwehr-dah deh sal-tahr*	skipping rope
la cuerda de volatinero	*lah kwehr-dah deh bohl-lah-teen-er-roh*	tightrope
el cuerno	*el kwehr-no*	horn
el cuerpo humano	*el kwehr-po oo-ma-noh*	body
la culebra	*lah koo-leh-brah*	snake
el dado	*el dah-doe*	dice
la dama de honor	*lah dah-mah-deh oh-nore*	bridesmaid
debajo/debaja	*deh-bah-gho/ deh-bah-ghah*	under
el dedo	*el deh-doe*	finger
el dedo del pie	*el deh-doe del pyeh*	toe
el delantal	*el deh-lahn-tahl*	apron
el delfín	*el dell-feen*	dolphin
delgado	*dell-gah-doe*	thin
el demonio	*el deh-moh-nee-yoh*	demon
el dentista	*el den-tees-tah*	dentist
dentro	*den-troh*	in
el deporte	*el deh-poor-teh*	sport
a la derecha	*ah lah deh-reh-chah*	right
el desayuno	*el dah-sah-ee-yoo-no*	breakfast
el desierto	*el deh-see-yehr-toe*	desert
el destornillador	*el des-tor-nee-lyah-door*	screwdriver
el detergente	*el deh-tehr-ghen-teh*	washing powder
el dibujo	*el dee-boo-gho*	drawing
diecinueve	*dee-yeh-thee-nweh-beh*	nineteen

Spanish	Pronunciation	English
ieciocho	dee-yeh-thee-oh-cho	eighteen
ieciséis	dee-yeh-thee-seh-eese	sixteen
iecisiete	dee-yeh-thee-syeh-teh	seventeen
l diente	el dyen-teh	tooth
iez	dee-yeth	ten
ifícil	dee-fee-theel	difficult
a diligencia	lah dee-lee-ghen-thee-ya	stagecoach
dinero	el dee-neh-ro	money
l dinosaurio	el dee-noh-sah-oo-ree-yo	dinosaur
l director de circo	el dee-rek-tore deh theer-ko	ringmaster
l director de orquesta	el dee-rek-tore deh or-kes-tah	conductor
l disco	el dees-ko	record
disfraz	el dees-frath	costume
oce	doh-theh	twelve
l domador de leones	el do-mah-door deh leh-yoh-ness	lion tamer
ormir	door-meer	to sleep
os	dose	two
dragon	el drah-gohn	dragon
a ducha	lah doo-chah	shower
l duende	el dwehn-deh	elf
l dulce de crema	el dool-theh deh kreh-mah	trifle (pudding)
uro/dura	doo-roh/doo-rah	hard
l edredón	el eh-dreh-dohn	eiderdown
l elefante	el eh-leh-fahn-teh	elephant
mpujar	ehm-pooh-ghahr	to push
l enano	el eh-nah-no	dwarf
ncima	en-thee-mah	over
a enfermera	lah en-fair-meh-rah	nurse
a ensalada	lah en-sah-lah-dah	salad
enyesado	el en-yeh-sah-doe	plaster
l equilibrista	el eh-kee-lee-bree-stah	trick cyclist, tightrope walker
a equitación	la eh-kee-tah-thyone	riding
erizo	el eh-ree-tho	hedgehog
a escalera de mano	lah eh-skah-leh-rah deh mah-no	ladder
a escala de cuerda	lah ehs-kah-lah deh kwehr-dah	rope ladder
as escaleras	'ahs ehs-kah-leh-rahs	stairs
l escalón	el eh-skah-lone	step
a escoba	lah ehs-koh-bah	broom, broomstick
sconderse	eh-skone-dehr-seh	to hide
a escopeta	lah eh-skoh-peh-tah	gun
scribir	eh-skree-beer	to write
scuchar	eh-skoo-chahr	to listen
a escudilla	lah eh-skoo-dee-lyah	bowl
a escuela	lah eh-skweh-lah	school
a espada	lah eh-spah-dah	sword
a espalda	lah eh-spahl-dah	back
l espantapájaros	el eh-spahn-tah-pah-ghah-rohs	scarecrow
l espejo	el eh-speh-gho	mirror
sperar	eh-speh-rahr	to wait
as espinacas	lahs eh-spee-nah-kas	spinach
a esponja	lah eh-spohn-ghah	sponge
a esposa	lah eh-spoh-sah	wife
l esposo	el eh-spoh-so	husband
a espuma de baño	lah eh-spoo-mah deh bah-nyo	bubbles
l esquí	el eh-skee	ski
l esquiador acuático	el eh-skee-yah-door ah-kwa-tee-ko	water skier
l establo	el eh-stah-blo	cowshed
a estación de ferrocarril	lah eh-stah-thyone- deh feh-roh-kah-reel	railway staion
as estaciónes	lahs eh-stah-thyo-nehs	seasons
star de pie	eh-star deh pyeh	to stand
star sentados	eh-star sen-tah-dos	to sit
a estatua	lah eh-stah-too-ah	statue
a esterilla	lah eh-steh-ree-lya	mat
estirar	eh-stee-rahr	to pull
el estómago	el eh-stoh-mah-go	tummy
la estrella	lah eh-streh-lya	star
la estrella de mar	lah eh-streh-lya deh mahr	starfish
la excavadora	lah eks-kah-bah-doh-rah	digger
la fábrica	lah fah-bree-kah	factory
fácil	fah-seel	easy
la falda	lah fahl-dah	skirt
la familia	lah fah-mee-lyah	family
el fantasma	el fahn-tah-smah	ghost
el faro	el fah-ro	lighthouse
el farol	el fah-role	lamp post
feo/fea	feh-oh/feh-ah	nasty
la feria	lah feh-ree-yah	fairground
los fideos	lohs fee-deh-yohs	spaghetti
la fiesta	lah fyeh-stah	party
la flecha	lah fleh-chah	arrow
la flor	lah floor	flower
la foca	lah foh-kah	seal
la forma	lah for-mah	shape
la foto	lah foh-toe	photograph
la frambuesa	lah frahm-bweh-sah	raspberry
el fregadero	el freh-gah-deh-ro	sink
el fregasuelos	el freh-gah-sweh-lohs	mop
la fresa	lah freh-sah	strawberry
frio/fria	free-yoh/free-yah	cold
la fruta	lah froo-tah	fruit
el fuego	el fweh-go	fire
los fuegos artificiales	lohs fweh-gose art-ee-feeth-ee-yah-lehs	fireworks
fuera	fwehr-rah	out
el fuerte	el fwehr-teh	fort
la furgoneta	lah foor-goh-neh-tah	van
el fútbol	el foot-bole	football
la galleta	lah gah-lyeh-tah	biscuit
la gallina	lah gah-lyee-nah	hen
el gallinero	el gah-lyee-neh-roe	henhouse
el gallo	el gah-lyoh	cock
ganar	gah-nahr	to win
el garaje	el gah-rah-gheh	garage
la gasolinera	lah gah-soh-lee-neh-rah	petrol station
el gatito	el gah-tee-toe	kitten
el gato	el gah-toe	cat
la gaviota	lah gah-bee-yoh-tah	seagull
la gente	lah ghehn-teh	people
el gigante	el ghee-gahn-teh	giant
la gimnasia	lah gheem-nah-syah	gymnastics
el globo	el gloh-bo	balloon
el globo terráqueo	el gloh-boh teh-rah-keh-yo	globe
la goma	lah go-ma	rubber
gordo/gorda	gore-do/gore-dah	fat
el gorila	el go-ree-lah	gorilla
la gorra	lah goh-rah	cap
la gráfica de temperaturas	lah grah-fee-kah deh tem-peh-rah-too-rahs	temperature chart
grande	grahn-deh	big
el granero	el grah-neh-ro	barn
la granja	lah grahn-ghah	farm
el granjero	el grahn-gheh-ro	farmer
el grifo	el gree-fo	tap
gris	greese	grey
la grúa	lah groo-wah	crane, breakdown lorry
el guante	el gwahn-teh	glove
el guardián del zoo	el gwar-dee-an del thoo	zoo keeper
el guardarropa	el gwahr-dah-roh-pah	wardrobe
la guirnalda de papel	lah geer-nahl-dah deh pah-pell	paper chain
los guisantes	lohs gee-sahn-tehs	peas
la guitarra	lah gee-tah-rah	guitar

Spanish	Pronunciation	English
el gusano	el goo-sah-no	worm
el gusano de seda	el goo-sah-noh deh seh-dah	silkworm
hablar	ah-blahr	to talk
hacer	ah-thehr	to make
hacer pompas	ah-thehr pohm-pahs	to blow
hacer punto	ah thehr poon-toe	to knit
el hacha	el ah-chah	axe
el hada	el ah-dah	fairy
el hámster	el ahm-stehr	hamster
la harina	lah ah-ree-nah	flour
la hebilla	lah ah-bee-lyah	buckle
la helada	lah eh-lah-dah	frost
el helado	el eh-lah-doe	ice cream
el helicóptero	el eh-lee-kop-teh-ro	helicopter
el heno	el eh-no	hay
la hermana	lah ehr-ma-nah	sister
el hermano	el ehr-ma-no	brother
la hierba	lah yehr-bah	grass
la hija	lah ee-ghah	daughter
el hijo	el ee-gho	son
el hipopótamo	el ee-po-po-ta-mo	hippopotamus
la hoguera	lah oh-geh-rah	bonfire
la hoja	lah oh-ghah	leaf
el hombre	el ohm-breh	man
el hombro	el ohm-bro	shoulder
la horca	lah or-kah	fork
la hormiga	lah or-mee-ga	ant
el hospital	el oh-spee-tal	hospital
el hotel	el oh-tell	hotel
el hoyo de arena	el oi-yoh deh ah-rain-ah	sandpit
la hucha	lah oo-chah	money box
el huerto	el where-toe	orchard
el hueso	el wheh-so	bone
el huevo	el wheh-boh	egg
el huevo frito	el wheh-boh free-toe	fried egg
el humo	el oo-moh	smoke
la iglesia	lah ee-gleh-syah	church
el indio	el een-dee-yo	Indian
el interruptor	el een-teh-roop-tore	switch
el invernadero	el een-behr-nah-deh-roh	greenhouse
el invierno	el een-byehr-no	winter
la inyección	lah een-yeck-thyone	syringe
el irrigador	el ee-ree-gah-door	sprinkler
la isla	lah ees-lah	island
a la izquierda	ah lah eeth-kyair-dah	left
el jabón	el ghah-bone	soap
la jalea	lah ghal-eh-ah	jelly
el jamón	el ghah-mone	ham
el jardín	el ghar-deen	garden
el jefe de estación	el gheh-feh deh eh-stah-thyone	station master
el jersey	el ghehr-seh	jumper
la jineta	lah ghee-neh-tah	bare-back rider
la jirafa	lah ghee-rah-fah	giraffe
las judías	lah ghoo-dee-yahs	beans
el judo	el ghoo-doe	judo
el juez	el ghweth	judge
jugar	ghoo-gar	to play
el juguete	el ghoo-geh-teh	toy
la juguetería	lah ghoo-get-eh-ree-ya	toy shop
el labio	el lah-bee-yo	lip
el ladrillo	el lah-dree-lyo	brick
el ladrón	el lah-drone	robber
el lago	el lah-go	lake
la lámpara	lah lahm-pa-rah	light
la lana	lah lah-nah	wool
la lancha de motor	lah lahn-chah deh moh-tore	speedboat
lanzar	lahn-thahr	to throw
el lápiz	el lah-peeth	pencil
el lápiz de colores	el lah-peeth deh koh-lore-ehs	crayon
el lagarto	el lah-gahr-to	lizard
largo/larga	lar-go/lar-gah	long
la lata	lah lah-tah	tin
el látigo	el lah-tee-go	whip
el lavabo	el lah-bah-do	wash basin
el lavado de coches	el lah-boh-doe deh koh-chehs	car wash
la lavadora	lah lah-bah-doh-rah	washing machine
lavarse	lah-bar-seh	to wash
lavarse los dientes	lah-bar-seh lohs dyen-tehs	to clean teeth
la leche	lah leh-cheh	milk
la lechuga	lah leh-choo-gah	lettuce
leer	leh-air	to read
la leña	lah len-ya	firewood
la lengua	lah len-gwah	tongue
lejos	leh-ghoss	far
lento	len-toe	slow
el león	el leh-yone	lion
el leopardo	el leh-oh-par-do	leopard
el levantamiento de pesos	el leh-bahn-tah-myen-toe des peh-sose	weightlifting
el libro	el lee-bro	book
la lima	lah lee-mah	file
el limón	el lee-mone	lemon
limpio/limpia	leem-pyoh/leem-pyah	clean
la linterna	lah leen-tair-nah	lantern
la llave	lah yah-beh	key
la llave inglesa	lah yah-beh een-gleh-sah	spanner
lleno/llena	lyeh-no/lyeh-na	full
llevar	lyeh-bar	to carry
llorar	lyoh-rar	to cry
la lluvia	lah lyoo-bee-yah	rain
el lobo	le loh-bo	wolf
el lodo	el loh-doe	mud
el loro	el loh-ro	parrot
la lucha libre	la loo-cha lee-breh	wrestling
la luna	lah loo-nah	moon
la luz delantera	la looth-deh-lahn-teh-rah	headlights
la luz de vengala	la looth deh ben-gah-lah	firework
el macizo de flores	el mah-thee-thoh-deh floh-rehs	flowerbed
la madera	lah ma-deh-rah	wood
la madre	lah ma-dreh	mother
mágico/mágica	ma-ghee-ko/ma-ghee-kah	magic
el mago	el mah-gho	wizard, magician
el malabarista	el mah-lah-bah-ree-stah	juggler
la maleta	lah ma-leh-tah	suitcase
malo/mala	ma-loh/ma-lah	bad
la manguera	lah mahn-geh-rah	hose
la mano	lah ma-no	hand
el mantel	el man-tell	tablecloth
la mantequilla	lah man-teh-kee-lyah	butter
la manzana	lah mahn-thah-nah	apple
el mapa	el ma-pah	map
la máquina	lah mah-kee-nah	engine
la máquina de escribir	lah mah-kee-nah deh eh-skree-beer	typewriter
la máquina fotográfica	lah mah-kee-nah foh-toh-grah-fee-kah	camera
el maquinista	el mah-kee-nee-stah	engine driver
el mar	el mar	sea
el marinero	el ma-ree-neh-ro	sailor
la marioneta	lah ma-ree-yoh-net-ah	puppet
la mariposa	lah ma-ree-poh-sah	butterfly
la mariposa nocturna	lah mah-ree-poh-sah nok-toor-nah	moth
marrón	ma-rone	brown
el martillo	el mahr-tee-lyo	hammer
la máscara	lah mah-skah-rah	mask
el matorral	el mah-toh-rahl	bush

Spanish	Pronunciation	English
l mecánico	el meh-kah-nee-koh	mechanic
ı media luna	lah meh-dyah loo-na	crescent
ıs medias	lahs meh-dee-yahs	tights
ıs medicinas	lahs meh-dee-thee-nahs	medicine
ı médico	el meh-dee-ko	doctor
ı mejilla	lah meh-ghee-lyah	cheek
l melocotón	el meh-lo-koh-tone	peach
ı melón	el meh-lone	melon
l mercado	el mehr-kah-doe	market
ı mermelada	lah mehr-meh-lah-dah	jam
ı mesa	lah mess-ah	table
ı mesita	lah meh-see-ta	small table
ı miel	lah myel	honey
ıirar	mee-rahr	to watch
ı mitad	lah mee-tahd	half
ıojado/mojada	moh-ghah-doh/ moh-ghah-dah	wet
l molino de viento	el moh-lee-noh deh byen-toe	windmill
ı monedero	el moh-neh-deh-ro	purse
ı mono	el moh-no	monkey
ı monstruo	el mone-stroo-oh	monster
ı montaña	lah mone-tah-nyah	mountain
ı montaña rusa	lah mone-tah-nyah roo-sah	big dipper
ıorado/morada	moh-rah-do/moh-rah-dah	purple
ı mosca	lah moh-skah	fly
ı motocicleta	lah moh-toh-thee-kleh-tah	motor cycle
ı motor	el moh-tore	engine
ıuchas	moo-chahs	a lot
ıuerto/muerta	mwere-toe/mwere-tah	dead
ı mujer	lah moo-ghair	woman
ıs muletas	lahs moo-leh-tahs	crutches
ı muñeca	lah moo-nyeh-kah	doll
ı murciélago	el moor-thee-yeh-lah-go	bat
ı naipe	el nah-ee-peh	playing card
ı naranja	lah nah-rahn-ghah	orange (fruit)
ı nariz	lah nah-reeth	nose
ı natación	lah nah-tah-thee-yohn	swimming
ı navaja	lah nah-bah-ghah	penknife
ı navegación	lah nah-beh-ghah-thee-yohn	sailing
ı neblina	lah neh-blee-nah	mist
egro/negra	neh-groh/neh-grah	black
l neumático	el neh-oo-mah-tee-ko	tyre
ı nevera	lah nehr-beh-rah	refrigerator
l nido de pájaro	el nee-doe deh pa-ghah-ro	nest
ı niebla	lah nyeh-blah	fog
ı nieve	lah nyeh-beh	snow
l niño	el nee-nyo	child
ı noria	lah no-ree-ya	big wheel
ı novia	lah no-bee-yah	bride
l novio	el no-bee-yo	bridegroom
ı nube	lah noo-beh	cloud
ıueve	nweh-beh	nine
ıuevo/nueva	nweh-boh/nweh-bah	new
ı nuez	lah noo-weth	nut
l número	el noo-meh-roh	number
ı oca	lah oh-kah	goose
ıcho	oh-cho	eight
l ojal	el oh-ghahl	buttonhole
l ojo	el oh-gho	eye
l ojo morado	el oh-gho moh-rah-doe	black eye
ı ola	lah oh-lah	wave
ınce	ohn-theh	eleven
ı oreja	lah oh-reh-ghah	ear
ı oruga	lah oh-roo-gah	caterpillar
ıscuro/oscura	oh-skoo-ro/oh-skoo-rah	dark
l osito de trapo	el oh-see-toh deh trah-po	teddy bear
l oso	el oh-so	bear
l oso blanco	el oh-so blahn-koh	polar bear

Spanish	Pronunciation	English
el otoño	el oh-toh-nyo	autumn
el óvalo	el oh-bah-loh	oval
la oveja	lah-oh-beh-ghah	sheep
el padre	el pa-dreh	father
el pajar	el pa-ghahr	loft
el pájaro	el pa-ghah-ro	bird
el paje	el pah-gheh	pageboy
la pajita	lah pah-ghee-tah	drinking straw
la pala	lah pa-la	spade
la palabra de acción	lah pa-la-bra deh ahk-theh-on	action word
la palabra de libros de cuentos	lah pa-la-bra deh lee-bross deh kwen-toss	story-book word
la palabra opuesta	lah pa-la-bra oh-pwehs-tah	opposite word
la palabra sobre el tiempo	lah pa-la-bra soh-breh el tyem-po	weather word
el palacio	el pah-lah-syo	palace
la paleta	lah pa-leh-tah	trowel
la paleta de tenis	lah pah-leh-tah deh teh-nees	bat, table tennis
el palo	el pah-loh	stick
la paloma	la pah-lo-ma	pigeon
las palomitas de maíz	lahs pah-lo-mee-tahs deh mah-eeth	popcorn
el pan	el pahn	bread
el panadero	el pah-nah-deh-ro	baker
el panda	el pahn-dah	panda
el panecillo	el pah-neh-thee-lyo	roll
los pantalones	los pahn-tah-loh-ness	trousers
los pantalones cortos	lohs pahn-tah-loh-ness kor-tose	shorts
el pañuelo	el pah-nyoo-weh-lo	handkerchief
el Papá Noel	el pah-pah no-ell	Father Christmas
el papel	el pah-pell	paper
el papel de lija	el pah-pell deh lee-ghah	sand paper
la papelera	lah pah-peh-leh-rah	wastepaper basket
el papel pintado	el pah-pell peen-tah-doh	wallpaper
el paquete	el pah-keh-teh	parcel
el paracaídas	el pah-rah-kah-yee-dahs	parachute
la pared	lah pah-red	wall
el parque	el par-keh	park
la parte delantera	lah par-teh deh-lahn-teh-rah	front
la parte trasera	lah par-teh trah-seh-rah	back
partir	par-teer	to chop
el paso de peatones	el pah-so deh peh-ya-tone-ess	pedestrian crossing
la pasta de dientes	lah pah-stah deh dyen-tess	toothpaste
el pastel	el pahs-tell	cake
el pastor	el pah-store	shepherd
la pata	lah pah-tah	paw
la patata	lah pah-tah-tah	potato
el patinaje	el pah-tee-nah-gheh	skating
el patin de ruedas	el pah-teen deh roo-weh-dahs	roller skate
el patinete	el pah-tee-neh-teh	scooter
el pato	el pah-toe	duck
el patio de recreo	el pah-tee-yo deh reh-kreh-yo	playground
el patito	el pah-tee-toe	duckling
el pavo	el pah-bo	turkey
el payaso	el pah-yah-so	clown
la pecera	lah peh-theh-rah	aquarium
el pecho	el peh-cho	chest
el peine	el peh-ee-neh	comb
pelear	peh-leh-yahr	to fight
el pelicano	el peh-lee-kah-no	pelican
el pelo	el peh-lo	hair
la pelota	lah peh-lo-ta	ball
pensar	pen-sahr	to think
el pepino	el pep-pee-no	cucumber

Spanish	Pronunciation	English	Spanish	Pronunciation	English
pequeño/ pequeña	peh-keh-nyoh/ peh-keh-nyah	small	el rabo	el rah-bo	tail
el periódico	el peh-ree-oh-dee-koh	newspaper	el radiador	el rah-dee-yah-door	radiator
el periquito	el peh-ree-kee-toh	budgerigar	la radio	lah rah-dee-yo	radio
el perro	el peh-ro	dog	el rail	el ray-yeel	railway line
el perro pastor	el peh-roh past-or	sheep dog	la rana	lah rah-nah	frog
la persiana	lah pehr-see-ya-na	window blind	rápido	rah-pee-do	fast
el pescado	el pess-kah-doe	fish	el rastrillo	el rah-stree-lyo	rake
el pescador	el pess-kah-dor	fisherman	el ratón	el rah-tone	mouse
el petrolero	el peh-troh-leh-ro	oil tanker	el recogedor del polvo	el reh-koh-gheh-dore del pole-bo	dustpan
el piano	el pyah-no	piano	la red	lah red	net
el picnic	el peek-neek	picnic	la red de seguridad	lah red deh seh-goo-ree-dahd	safety net
el pie	el pyeh	foot	el regalo	el reh-gah-lo	present
la piedra	lah pyeh-drah	stone	el relámpago	el reh-lahm-pah-go	lightning
la piedrecita	lah pyeh-dreh-thee-tah	pebble	la regla	lah reh-glah	ruler
la pierna	lah pyehr-nah	leg	la reina	lah reh-ee-nah	queen
el pijama	el pee-ghah-ma	pyjama	reírse	reh-eer-seh	to laugh
la píldora	lah peel-doh-rah	pill	el reloj	el reh-logh	clock, watch
el piloto	el pee-lote-oh	pilot	el remo	el reh-mo	oar, rowing
la pimienta	lah pee-mee-yen-tah	pepper	el remolque	el reh-mole-keh	trailer
la piña	lah pee-nyah	pineapple	el renacuajo	el reh-nah-kwah-gho	tadpole
el pincel	el peen-sell	brush	el reno	el reh-no	reindeer
el ping-pong	el peen-pon	table tennis	el retrete	el reh-treh-teh	toilet
el pingüino	el peen-gwee-no	penguin	el revisor	el reh-bee-sore	ticket collector
pintar	peen-tahr	to paint	el rey	el reh-ee	king
el pintor	el peen-tore	painter	el rinoceronte	el ree-no-theh-rohn-teh	rhinoceros
la pintura	lah peen-too-rah	paint	el río	el ree-yo	river
el pirata	el pee-rah-tah	pirate	el robot	el roh-boat	robot
el piso	el pee-so	flat	la roca	la roh-kah	rock
la pista de aterrizaje	lah pee-stah deh ah-teh-ree-thah-gheh	runway	el rocío	el roh-thee-yo	dew
la pistola	la pee-stoh-lah	pistol	la rodilla	lah roh-dee-lyah	knee
la pizarra	lah pee-thah-rah	blackboard	rojo/roja	roh-gho/roh-ghah	red
la placa	lah plah-kah	badge	el rombo	el rome-boh	diamond
la plancha	lah plahn-chah	iron	el rompecabezas	el rome-peh-kah-beh-thahs	jigsaw
la planta	lah plahn-tah	plant			
el plátano	el plah-tah-no	banana	romper	rome-pehr	to break
el platito	el plah-tee-toe	saucer	la rueda	lah roo-weh-dah	wheel
el plato	el plah-toh	plate			
la playa	lah plah-ee-yah	beach, seaside	la sábana	lah sah-bah-nah	sheet
la pluma	lah ploo-mah	pen	el saco	el sah-ko	sack
la pocilga	lah poh-theel-gah	pig sty	la sal	lah sahl	salt
pocas	po-cahs	little	la salchicha	lah sahl-chee-chah	sausage
la policía	lah poh-lee-thee-ya	policeman	la salsa	lah sahl-sah	sauce
el pollito	el poh-lyee-toe	chick	saltar	sahl-tahr	to jump, to skip
el pollo	el poh-lyo	chicken	el salto de altura	el sahl-toh deh ahl-too-rah	high jump
el pomo de la puerta	el poh-moh deh lah pwer-tah	door handle	las sandalias	lahs sahn-dah-lee-yahs	sandals
el pony	el po-nee	pony	el sapo	el sah-po	toad
el portaequipajes	el poor-tah-eh-kee-pah-gheh	boot (of car)	la sartén	lah sahr-ten	frying pan
			seco/seca	seh-koh/seh-kah	dry
el portero	el poor-tehr-oh	porter	seis	seh-eese	six
el poste indicador	el poh-steh een-dee-kah-dore	signpost	el semáforo	el seh-mah-foh-roh	traffic lights
			la semilla	lah seh-mee-lyah	seed
el pote	el poh-teh	jar	la señal	lah seh-nyal	signal
el pozo	el po-tho	well	el sendero	el sen-deh-ro	path
la prima	lah pree-mah	cousin (female)	el serrín	el seh-reen	sawdust
la primavera	lah pree-mah-beh-rah	spring	la seta	lah seh-tah	mushroom
el primero	el pree-mah-ro	first	el seto	el seh-toh	hedge
el primo	el pree-mo	cousin (male)	el sheriff	el sheh-reef	sheriff
la princesa	lah preen-theh-sah	princess	la sierra	lah see-air-rah	saw
el príncipe	el preen-theeh-peh	prince	siete	syeh-teh	seven
la profesora	lah pro-fess-or-ah	teacher	el silbato	el seel-bah-toe	whistle
el pueblo	el pweh-blo	village	la silla	la see-lyah	chair
el puente	el pwen-teh	bridge	la silla de montar	lah see-lyah deh mohn-tahr	saddle
el puerro	el pweh-ro	leek			
la puerta	lah pwer-tah	door	la silla de ruedas	lah see-lyee deh roo-weh-dahs	wheelchair
la puerta de esclusa	lah pwehr-tah deh eh-skloo-sah	lock (canal)	la sillita de ruedas	lah see-lee-tah deh roo-weh-dahs	pushchair
el puerto	el pwer-toe	harbour	el sol	el sohl	sun
el pulgar	el pool-gahr	thumb	el soldadito de plomo	el sole-dah-dee-toh deh ploh-mo	toy soldier
el pupitre	el poo-pee-tray	desk	el soldado	el sole-dah-doe	soldier
el queso	el keh-so	cheese	el sombrero	el sohm-breh-roh	hat
quince	keen-theh	fifteen	el sombrero de paja	el sohm-breh-roh deh pah-ghah	straw hat
el quitasol	el kee-tah-sol	umbrella			

Spanish	Pronunciation	English
sombrero de papel	*el sohm-breh-roh deh pah-pell*	paper hat
reír	*sohn-reh-yeer*	to smile
sopa	*lah so-pa*	soup
submarinista	*el soob-mah-ree-nee-stah*	frogman
submarino	*el soob-mah-ree-no*	submarine
cio/sucia	*soo-thyoh/soo-thyah*	dirty
suelo	*el sweh-lo*	floor
suéter	*el sweh-tehr*	sweater
supermercado	*el soo-pehr-mehr-kah-doe*	supermarket
surtidor de gasolina	*el soor-tee-dore deh gah-soh-lee-nah*	petrol pump
tabla de planchar	*lah tah-blah deh plahn-chahr*	ironing board
tablón	*el tah-blone*	plank
taburete	*el tah-boo-reh-teh*	stool
tachuela	*lah tah-chweh-lah*	tack
taladradora	*lah tah-lah-drah-doh-rah*	road drill
taladro	*el tah-lah-dro*	drill
taller	*el tah-lyehr*	workshop
talón	*el tah-lone*	heel
tambor	*el tahm-bore*	drum
tanque	*el tahn-keh*	tank
taxi	*el tahk-see*	taxi
taza	*lah tah-thah*	cup
té	*el teh*	tea
tebeo	*el teh-beh-yo*	comic
techo	*el teh-choh*	ceiling
tejado	*el teh-ghah-doe*	roof
tejanos	*lohs teh-ghah-nohs*	jeans
tejón	*el teh-ghone*	badger
teleraña	*lah teh-leh-rah-nyah*	cobweb
teléfono	*el teh-leh-foh-no*	telephone
televisión	*la teh-leh-bee-see-yone*	television
tendero	*el ten-deh-ro*	shopkeeper
tenedor	*el teh-neh-door*	fork
tenis	*el teh-nees*	tennis
termómetro	*el tehr-moh-meh-tro*	thermometer
ternero	*el tehr-neh-ro*	calf
tesoro	*el teh-sor-ro*	treasure
tía	*lah tee-yah*	aunt
tiburón	*el tee-boo-rone*	shark
tiempo	*el tyem-po*	weather
tienda	*lah tyen-dah*	shop
tienda de campaña	*lah tyehn-dah-deh kahm-pah-nyah*	tent
tierra	*lah tyeh-rah*	earth
tigre	*el tee-greh*	tiger
tijeras	*lahs tee-gheh-rahs*	scissors
tío	*el tee-yo*	uncle
tiovivo	*el tee-yoh-bee-bo*	roundabout
ar	*tee-rahr*	to pull
tiro al blanco	*el tee-ro ahl blahn-ko*	shooting
titere	*el tee-teh-reh*	puppet
tiza	*lah tee-thah*	chalk
toalla	*lah toe-ah-ee-lyah*	towel
tobogán	*el toe-boh-gahn*	helter-skelter, slide
tocadiscos	*el toh-kah-deese-kose*	record player
do	*toe-do*	whole
mar	*toe-mahr*	to take
tomate	*el toe-mah-teh*	tomato
tope	*el toe-peh*	buffer
topo	*el toe-po*	mole
tornillo	*el tor-nee-lyo*	screw
tornillo a tuerca	*el tor-nee-lyo ah twer-kah*	bolt
torno de banco	*el tor-no deh bahn-ko*	vice
toronja	*lah toh-rohn-ghah*	grapefruit
toro	*el toh-roh*	bull
torre de control	*lah toh-reh deh kohn-trole*	control tower
tortilla	*lah tohr-tee-lyah*	omelette
tortita	*lah tohr-tee-tah*	pancake
la tortuga	*lah tohr-too-gah*	tortoise
el tractor	*el trak-tohr*	tractor
el traje de baño	*el trah-gheh deh bah-nyoh*	swimsuit
el trapecio	*el trah-peh-thee-yo*	trapeze
el trapo	*el trah-poh*	duster
el trasero	*el trah-seh-ro*	bottom (body)
trece	*treh-theh*	thirteen
el tren	*el trehn*	train
el tren de mercancías	*el trehn deh mehr-kahn-thee-yahs*	goods train
el tren fantasma	*el trehn fahn-tahs-mah*	ghost train
trepar	*treh-par*	to climb
tres	*trehs*	three
el triángulo	*el tree-ahn-goo-lo*	triangle
el trigo	*el tree-go*	corn
el trineo	*el tree-neh-oh*	sleigh
la trompa	*lah trome-pah*	trunk
la trompeta	*lah trome-peh-tah*	trumpet
el tronco	*el trone-koh*	log
la tubería	*lah too-beh-ree-ya*	pipe
la tuerca	*lah twehr-kah*	nut
la tumbona	*lah toom-bone-ah*	deckchair
el túnel	*el too-nell*	tunnel
ultimo	*ool-tee-moh*	last
uno/una	*oo-noh/oo-nah*	one
la uva	*lah oo-bah*	grape
la vaca	*lah bah-kah*	cow
vacio/vacia	*bah-thee-yoh/bah-thee-yah*	empty
el vagón	*el bah-gohn*	carriage
el vagón restaurante	*el bah-gohn res-tah-oo-rahn-teh*	buffet car
la valla	*lah bah-lyah*	railings, fence
el vaquero	*el bah-keh-ro*	cowboy
la vara	*lah bah-rah*	pole
la varita mágica	*lah bah-ree-tah mah-ghee-kah*	wand
el vaso	*el bah-so*	glass (drinking)
veinte	*beh-een-teh*	twenty
la vela	*lah beh-lah*	candle
la venda	*lah ben-dah*	bandage
la ventana	*lah ben-tah-nah*	window
el verano	*el bah-rah-no*	summer
verde	*behr-deh*	green
las verduras	*lahs behr-doo-rahs*	vegetables
el vestido	*el bes-tee-doe*	dress
los vestidos	*lohs beh-stee-dose*	clothes
viejo/vieja	*byeh-ghoh/byeh-ghah*	old
el viento	*el byen-toe*	wind
el vino	*el bee-no*	wine
las virutas	*lahs bee-roo-tahs*	shavings
vivo/viva	*bee-boh/bee-bah*	alive
el volatinero	*el boh-lah-tee-neh-ro*	tight-rope walker
el yate	*el yah-teh*	yacht
el yogur	*el yoh-goor*	yoghurt
la zanahoria	*lah thah-nah-or-ee-yah*	carrot
la zapatilla	*lah thah-pah-tee-lyah*	slipper
la zapatilla de goma	*lah thah-pah-tee-lyah deh goh-mah*	gym shoe
los zapatos	*lohs thah-pah-tose*	shoes
la zebra	*lah theh-brah*	zebra
el zoo	*el thoo*	zoo
el zorrito	*el thoh-ree-to*	fox cub
el zorro	*el thoh-ro*	fox
el zumo	*el thoo-mo*	squash
el zumo de naranja	*el thoo-moh deh nah-rahn-ghah*	orange juice